Superhero

Sailor

Baby
Dress
Up

Musician

Elephant

Pilot

Baseball Player

Cheerleader

Dinosaur

Lion

Chef

Safari Guide

Pumpkin

Bear

Princess

Bunny

Mechanic

Watermelon

Puppy

Snail

Skeleton

Elephant

Bunny

Wate[illegible]on

Your baby will love to see other babies just like them dressed up in silly, adorable, and cuddly costumes in this colorful book made just for baby!

Collect the entire Baby Firsts series:
Look What I Can Do! • W[illegible] Baby's Feelings • Baby's Day
Baby's Favorite Things [illegible] Watch Me Grow!

SRP: $6.99 USD
9 781486 714612

Flowerpot Press
"Planting the seeds that help young minds grow."
TORONTO • NASHVILLE
www.FlowerpotPress.com
FBB-0707-0352 · 978-1-4867-1461-2
Made in China/Fabriqué en Chine DS-4703